G.O.A.T.

MAKING THE CASE FOR THE GREATEST OF ALL TIME

SIMONE BILES

BY SUSAN BLACKABY

STERLING CHILDREN'S BOOKS
New York

STERLING CHILDREN'S BOOKS
New York

An Imprint of Sterling Publishing Co., Inc.
1166 Avenue of the Americas
New York, NY 10036

ISBN 978-1-4549-3206-2

Distributed in Canada by Sterling Publishing Co., Inc.
c/o Canadian Manda Group, 664 Annette Street
Toronto, Ontario M6S 2C8, Canada
Distributed in the United Kingdom by GMC Distribution Services
Castle Place, 166 High Street, Lewes, East Sussex BN7 1XU, England
Distributed in Australia by NewSouth Books
45 Beach Street, Coogee, NSW 2034, Australia

For information about custom editions, special sales, and premium
and corporate purchases, please contact Sterling Special Sales at
800-805-5489 or specialsales@sterlingpublishing.com.

Manufactured in China
Lot #:
2 4 6 8 10 9 7 5 3 1
08/19

sterlingpublishing.com

Cover and interior design by Heather Kelly

Image credits are on page 127

I'd rather regret the risks that didn't work out
than the chances I didn't take at all.
—Simone Biles

CONTENTS

INTRODUCTION: WHAT IS A G.O.A.T?

Most people do not want to be compared to a barnyard animal, but a G.O.A.T. is different. These G.O.A.T.'s aren't found on farms or in petting zoos. They are at the gym and on the gridiron, the hardwood, the ice, and the diamond. G.O.A.T. is an acronym that stands for Greatest of All Time. It takes lifelong dedication, non-stop hard work, and undeniable talent just to become a professional athlete. But to become the Greatest of All Time, well, that's nearly impossible. Only a handful of athletes across the sporting world are widely thought to be the G.O.A.T. Swimmer Michael Phelps moves like a fish in water, but he is also the G.O.A.T. with 28 gold medals, more than any other Olympian. Tennis great Serena Williams is the G.O.A.T. with 23 Grand Slam titles in the Open Era—more than any other player, woman or man.

For some sports, the G.O.A.T. is not as easy to identify, and fans may disagree. Ask five baseball lovers who the greatest baseball player of all time is, and you might get five different answers: Babe Ruth, Willie Mays, Barry Bonds, Cy Young, Lou Gehrig, or the up-and-coming Shohei Ohtani or Juan Soto. The G.O.A.T. can change depending on who is asked and what their reasons, or criteria, are. Babe Ruth won seven World Series, had a career batting average of .342, and is still in 3rd place among the all-time home-run hitters even though he retired over 80 years ago in 1935. Willie Mays did not have Ruth's high batting stats, but he is still considered to be the best defensive player in history. Different players, different achievements, but still the greatest at what they did. Fans will disagree on who the G.O.A.T. is, but in order to even be considered, an athlete must be one of the best to ever live.

Women's gymnastics has its own set of standards and standouts when it comes to naming the G.O.A.T. Olga Korbut literally gave the sport a new twist with her back flip on the balance beam at the Munich Olympics in 1972. At the Montreal games in 1976, Nadia Comăneci was the first gymnast to score a perfect 10 in an Olympic gymnastics event. At the 1984 Olympic Games in Los Angeles, Mary Lou Retton was the first American female gymnast to win a gold medal. And don't forget the Magnificent Seven at the 1996 games in

Atlanta. Kerri Strug competed with a severely sprained ankle to help Team USA come out on top. These women and many others have pushed the limits of a difficult and demanding sport. But Simone Biles? She has propelled it straight up into the stratosphere. Could she be the G.O.A.T.? You decide.

A gymnast's second home

1

FINDING FAMILY

You never know how plain old chance will change your life forever. For Simone Biles, it was bad weather and a cancelled field trip. On a rainy summer morning, the day care center that Simone and her little sister, Adria, attended was supposed to have a field day to visit a farm. Their older brother Adam, who worked at the center, quickly came up with a dry and easy Plan B. He took the kids down the street to Bannon's Gymnastix instead, and the rest is history.

Almost.

At the gym, six-year-old Simone instantly felt right at home. She watched the gymnasts vaulting and cartwheeling, spinning and flipping, and she couldn't contain her excitement. She wanted to copy the gymnasts' every move and try out every piece of equipment, or **appara-tus**—bars, beams, **springboards**, and mats. Simone had already spent a lot of her short life airborne—bouncing on beds, jumping on trampolines, bounding from bunks, scrambling up to perch on her brothers' shoulders—twirling through space on her way back to the ground.

Catching up to Simone as she bounced around the gym, Adam challenged her to do a back flip. Simone told Adam to go first and laughed when he crash-landed. Then it was her turn. Simone already had a knack for back flips, but she'd never gotten to do them on a springy floor before.

Sproing! Sproing! Sproing!

Showing off for Adam, Simone even added a little twist as she stuck every landing. It turned out that Adam wasn't the only person watching. One of the coaches approached as Simone landed another flip. The coach asked Adam if Simone had had any formal training and suggested that she sign up for a class. Simone left the gym that day with an invitation to enroll.

Momma Biles was not that impressed. She assumed that every kid came home with a flyer. Then she got to thinking about her energetic little ones tumbling around the house. Maybe the gym was worth a try after all. Simone and Adria were soon signed up to attend classes twice a week.

The first class had hardly begun when the coach knew without a shadow of a doubt that Simone had a special gift for gymnastics. Just like that, she had landed in exactly the right place.

It wasn't the first time.

A ROCKY START

Simone Biles was born March 14, 1997, in Columbus, Ohio. Her older sister, Ashley, was seven years old, and her brother Tevin was three. By the time Adria was born two years later, Simone's home life had started to unravel. Her single mother, Shanon Biles, was having a hard time taking care of herself, let alone her family. Social Services stepped in and put the four children into foster care.

Simone was just three years old, and although she recalls understanding exactly what it meant to have her family broken apart, she has held on to only a few memories of her foster parents. She remembers their kindness and their care and their patience. She remembers their swing set, which sent her sailing through the air as she copied Tevin's daredevil flips and twirls. She remembers their trampoline, which she wasn't allowed to play on for fear she'd get hurt. And she remembers the day her grandfather, Shanon's father, showed up to take Simone and her brother and sisters home—home to Texas, where he lived with his family.

Simone's grandfather Ron Biles, a retired Air Force sergeant, had a job working in air traffic control in Houston. Her grandmother Nellie Biles had a demanding career as a nurse. She had nearly raised her sons, Adam and Ron II, who were in high school. She was looking forward to a quiet household with no teenagers around when the social worker called from Ohio. The Biles grandkids needed help.

While Simone's grandfather attended to the legal details of bringing the children from Ohio to Texas, her grandmother worried. Nellie didn't know the kids as well as Ron did. He had visited them in Ohio many times over the years, but she had usually stayed home with her boys. Would she be able to give these children the love and support they needed? Nellie had been part of a large and close-knit family in Belize. She knew how important growing up with strong family connections could be. She wanted to be able to provide her grandchildren with rock-solid stability and trust. She dug deep to find the faith and courage it would take to meet the challenge.

Ron Biles arrived in Texas with the children in March 2000. Almost as soon as Simone was out of the car at the family home in Spring—a small community north of

Houston—she hopped onto the trampoline in the backyard. Sixteen-year-old Adam spotted her. Even as she flew through the air on that first exhilarating leap, Simone started to feel as if she were on solid ground.

FAMILY TIES

Simone and Adria were very attached to each other, and they soon became close to their grandparents as well. Simone didn't have many clear memories of living with their biological mother—and Adria didn't have any at all. But Tevin and Ashley missed Shanon terribly. The children had been living in Texas for eight months when Shanon came to visit them.

Simone felt shy trying to reconnect with her mother. When Shanon said she wanted the kids to come back to Ohio to live with her, Simone didn't know how to feel. She loved her grandparents, and she loved living in Spring. A social worker stepped in and said that the four Biles children needed to stay together, either in Texas or Ohio. What seemed best for the older kids would need to work for the younger ones, too. It wasn't long before Tevin and Ashley made their choice known, and so Ron Biles took the four children back to Ohio.

Instead of moving in with their mother as planned, the Biles children were placed back with their foster family. Shanon wasn't yet ready to care for them—and it turned out that she never would be. After a year of uncertainty, the four children were put up for adoption. Once again, their grandparents stepped in to help. Ron and Nellie wanted all four kids to come back to Texas, but Tevin and Ashley decided to stay behind in order to be closer to their mom. Ron's sister in Ohio adopted the two older kids. On December 24, 2002, Simone and Adria returned to Texas with their grandfather.

DAD AND MOM

In her time away from Texas, Simone hadn't lost any of her energy. The high level of bounce was familiar to her grandparents; but her quiet, guarded, protective side was new. The instability of her early years made it hard for Simone to understand what home and family even meant, and she wasn't sure she could trust that it would last. With time, love, and faith, her grandparents helped her learn—and they learned how to define their new family, too.

CONNECTIONS

Simone has contact with Shanon and with her Ohio siblings, but is grateful to be part of a close-knit, loving family in Texas.

On November 7, 2003, Ron and Nellie Biles formally and legally adopted Simone and Adria. From then on, the girls chose to call their grandparents Mom and Dad. Simone had landed in exactly the right place.

2

BEGINNING AT BANNON'S

Simone didn't even last a month in her new class at Bannon's Gymnastix. The coaches who worked with the little kids in the recreation program saw that Simone had something special—something that most kids don't have. Even for a six-year-old, she was teeny-tiny, but she was solid muscle and super strong. On one particular day, she was sitting with her legs straight out in front of her. She put her hands down at her sides and lifted her legs and hips up off the floor. This move, called an L-seat, is much harder than it looks. (You can try it yourself!) It takes ironclad core muscles most six-year-olds don't have—which is what caught coach Aimee Boorman's attention as she happened to be passing by. Aimee kept watching as Simone stood on a thick mat and did seat drops while she waited her turn in line. Aimee knew that nothing about Simone's remarkable energy, strength, and ability fell within the normal range for a kid her age; she didn't realize it would change both their lives.

MOVING UP

Simone's little sister, Adria, didn't like gymnastics. She quit the beginner class to join a Brownie troop and become a Girl Scout. Simone didn't like gymnastics, either. Simone *loved* gymnastics! Simone quit the beginner class to join Bannon's USA Gymnastics Junior Olympic program (**USAG JO**). The JO program puts young gymnasts on a track to move through ten set skill levels and compete in district, state, regional, and national competitions.

A few weeks after Simone joined Bannon's Jet Star team, as her JO group was called, parents and families came to watch the kids perform. One of the basic conditioning exercises was the seated rope climb. Children took turns sitting beside a dangling rope and pulling themselves up hand over hand using only their arms and upper-body strength. They were to climb about ten feet up the rope, keeping their legs stretched out straight in front of them. When it was Simone's turn, she easily pulled herself up to ten feet and then just kept on going,

Training to be a gymnast takes hours of conditioning.

higher and higher. She laughed, bobbing at the top of the rope like a balloon on a string.

When Simone started her JO program, she was put into Level 4, but was soon learning Level 5 skills, too. Even though Simone hadn't had any formal training, she already had a strong skill set thanks to playing with her brothers. Of course, she didn't know the exact steps to follow for each move, and her form was all over the place. She needed to add grace and control to her enthusiasm and ability, including pointed toes, artistic hand positions, and fully extended arms and legs.

NATURAL ABILITY

The coaches at Bannon's soon realized that Simone had been born with an extraordinary natural talent for gymnastics—one that could take her all the way to the Olympics. For example, Simone was able to learn new skills just by copying what she saw. She could watch a move and then quickly and easily figure out how to turn action into technique. She also had a critical skill called air sense. As Simone tumbles, spins, flips, twists, and flies through the air upside down and backward, she knows where she is in space so that she is able to land feet first and upright. (Think of a cat.) You can imagine how important air sense is for both safety and success as moves become more and more difficult. It plays a fundamental role, and it isn't something that can be taught.

Whatever Simone may have lacked in those early weeks and months of her training, she had two things going for her: she was fearless, and she couldn't wait to tackle and master each new skill. Being fearless doesn't mean that Simone didn't ever get scared. Learning big moves can be risky. Hard falls are not only painful, they can be frightening. But Simone's coaches worked to keep stumbling blocks from becoming mental blocks. They made her get right back up and work through a difficult move—whether she wanted to or not. (And there were plenty of times when stubborn Simone did *not*!) They helped Simone prove to herself that she could overcome any negative feelings—distress, panic, nerves, tension, pain—moving through failure to gain confidence, control, and success.

As Simone came to trust her coaches and her abilities, she was able to tap into a deep well of courage. She had the courage to try, the courage to fail, and the courage to try again. You don't get to be the G.O.A.T. without it.

3

REQUIREMENTS AND RANKINGS

USA Gymnastics sets all the rules for gymnastics training and competition in the United States. It is also in charge of the Junior Olympic program.

JUNIOR OLYMPICS

 In 2017, there were 67,000 girls enrolled in the JO program nationwide.

Girls in the Junior Olympic program go through ten levels of training. Each level has a set of requirements that every gymnast must complete. Mastering each skill before moving on helps maintain standards. It also helps make sure gymnasts are safely prepared as they attempt harder and harder moves.

Gymnasts at Levels 4 through 6 all perform the exact same routines mapped out by USAG. These moves reflect the basic skills and combinations that every gymnast must be able to do on each apparatus—**vault, bars, beam, floor**.

THE EQUIPMENT

These are the four types of equipment women use in gymnastics:

 Vault—a short runway, springboard, and padded "vault table" that is 4 feet off the floor. The gymnast performs a series of **aerial moves** before landing.

 Uneven Bars—two parallel, horizontal bars set 6 feet apart; one is 5'4" off the ground, the other is 8 feet off the ground. In 90 seconds, the gymnast must **mount**, leap, jump, flip, turn, and **dismount**, flowing from one move to the next.

 Balance Beam—a beam about 16 feet long and 4 inches wide set 4 feet off the ground; turns, jumps, handstands, and flips are executed as if the gymnast were on the floor.

 Floor—a square mat that is 40 feet by 40 feet; the gymnast has 90 seconds to combine elements of dance with tumbling passes set to music.

Men's gymnastics differs from women's in the type of equipment that is used, and men do six events instead of four: floor, vault, parallel bars, horizontal bar, still rings, and pommel horse.

Gymnasts progress through the JO training at their own pace. They move up from one level to the next by achieving a minimum score at competitions. Gymnasts can't skip levels. They can compete in more than one level as long as they meet the age requirement, but they can't compete in more than two meets per year.

In the gymnastics world, Simone was getting off to a late start as she turned seven. She needed to make up for lost time. Typically, girls begin Level 1 at age four and work their way up. In theory, you have to be at least nine years old to compete at Level 10, but achieving that level before a gymnast reaches her teens is very rare. Some coaches recommend slowing down the pace as girls compete at higher levels. They favor setting realistic goals that will be safe and healthy. They allow time for gymnasts to gain maturity, and they help them avoid burnout.

•   •   •

SCORING BASICS

The current gymnastics scoring handbook is more than 25 pages long, and you can imagine that the information gets pretty technical. Up until 2006, gymnasts were scored on a 10-point scale. Now judges use the following guidelines:

- Points are awarded for four special requirements that must be met at each level.

- Points are awarded for the amount of difficulty and technical ability. Each skill from beginning to advanced has been assigned a value, and a certain amount of difficulty is required as a gymnast progresses from level to level. There isn't any limit to the number of points a gymnast can earn for difficulty and technical ability.

- Points are awarded for execution and artistry, which includes the dismount. The maximum number of points for this aspect of a routine is 10 points.

- Points are awarded on some apparatuses for connection value, which refers to skills executed successfully in a sequence.

- Points are deducted for errors, which can range from 0.1 point off for a small wobble to 1.0 point off for a fall.

- After those scores are tallied, "neutral deductions" are subtracted for errors such as stepping out of bounds, going over the time limit on a routine, breaking any clothing or behavior rules, and so on, to get the individual score. At the **elite** level, anything above 15 points puts a gymnast within striking distance of a medal.

- Individual scores are added together to get an all-around score.

- Team scores are determined by adding up the top three individual scores for each event.

APPARATUS OVERVIEW

Female gymnasts showcase their skills on the vault, bars, beam, and floor. A gymnast does not need to compete on all four apparatuses unless she wants to qualify as an all-around champion.

Vault

The vault is broken into sections: the *run*, when the gymnast runs toward the springboard; the *hurdle*—hitting the springboard from one foot, two feet, or a handspring; the *pre-flight*, which takes the gymnast from contact with the springboard to the vault table; *contact with the table*, which the gymnast pushes off of with as much

Hitting the mat without moving your feet or taking a hop is called sticking the landing.

force as possible in order to gain height and momentum; the *post-flight*, during which the gymnast performs flips and twists; and the *landing*, which must be completed within a designated area without moving the feet.

Uneven Bars

Skills on the uneven bars include release moves, turns, and circles. Release moves involve letting go of the bar and then grasping it again. Turns involve using the hands to change position while holding a handstand. Circles are 360° rotations performed either in a handstand position or with the hips close to the bar. A bar routine includes fifteen or twenty moves, flowing from one move to the next and using both the high bar and the low bar. Acrobatic moves including flips and twists are part of the dismount.

Uneven bars require nerves of steel.

Balance Beam

Look around you to find objects that are about four inches wide—a library card or a business envelope is about right, but a cell phone and a postcard, for example, are wider. Along this narrow rail, a gymnast performs a complex routine that includes leaps, jumps, turns, holds, and acrobatics.

In a leap, the gymnast propels off one foot, does splits in midair, and lands on one foot; the split must be 180° to

Simone is known for her amazing splits.

earn full marks. Variations make the leap more difficult, including a switch leap, in which the front leg is scissored back, or a ring leap, in which the heel of the back leg is brought up toward the head. Jumps begin on two feet and land on two feet. Air positions and twists add to the level of difficulty. To turn, the gymnast must spin on one foot. The turn must be at least 360°, but the more revolutions, the higher the score. Holds include moves such as handstands. These are done in combination with other parts of the routine so that they don't take up too much time.

Acrobatic moves include forward and backward walkovers, handsprings, and somersaults or flips (called **saltos**). Difficulty increases with added twists, multiple rotations, and body positions (**tuck** or **layout**). The mount—getting onto the beam—and dismount—getting off the beam and landing on the ground without moving the feet—can be the most technically demanding and complicated (as well as dangerous) parts of the entire routine.

The Floor Exercise

The floor exercise combines dance skills, which are similar to skills performed on the balance beam, and four or five tumbling passes. Tumbling passes include com-

A winning floor exercise must be both athletic and artistic.

binations of multiple flips and twists, staying within the bounds of the mat and sticking every landing.

MAKING PROGRESS

To qualify as an all-around gymnast, Simone trained on every apparatus, and her coaches quickly got her up to Level 6. In addition to conditioning, they shaped and tailored moves Simone could already do. They instructed her on how to execute moves that were new to her. And they helped her work through moves that took her outside her comfort zone.

Simone herself has admitted that from the beginning she had problems with the uneven bars. They can be tricky to master for a power gymnast. A power gymnast is used to controlling an apparatus, using the equipment to help gain height and spring for flips and twists. The bars are different: they dictate the gymnast's movements, and along the way they can be scary. Simone is a small person (4'8") with small hands. Everything about the bars tests her freak-out level!

Did Simone have to be good at all four events? Not necessarily. Plenty of gymnasts specialize on a certain apparatus, concentrating on excellence in one over another. Simone would have been willing to skip the bars altogether, but her coaches persuaded her to keep trying. They believed that Simone could become an all-around champion, but it would require mastering all four events. Step 1 is having confidence. Step 2 is building confidence. Being able to do full rotations while fully **extended** on the high bar—a move called a giant—is required if you want to compete on the uneven bars at Level 6. With guidance and hours and hours of practice, Simone managed to bridge the gap between struggle and success. She was able to perform giants with ease for the Level 6 competition.

Once gymnasts reach Level 7, they move from required skills to acquired skills. They are able to build on the basics and add optional combinations to create their own routines. This not only showcases strengths, it increases the level of difficulty, which can translate into higher scores. It also means competing in the larger state and regional meets. These meets are more nerve-racking, involve more top-flight competitors, and offer more exposure. At Bannon's, Aimee Boorman was the coach in charge of working with gymnasts in Level 7 and up. She took over Simone's training.

COACH AIMEE BOORMAN

Aimee Banghart Boorman was born in Chicago. She started gymnastics at age seven through Chicago Parks and Rec, and then continued at Lakeshore Academy of Artistic Gymnastics. She began coaching at age 13 to help pay for her training. She won a city championship in the floor exercise when she was a freshman in high school and competed all four years.

Aimee entered Northern Illinois University in 1991 to study sports business, but she was soon back in the gym, teaching gymnastics part-time. In 1995 on a trip to Texas, Aimee landed a coaching job; ten years later, she met Simone.

As Simone developed her skills, Aimee had to develop her coaching philosophy and expand her scope. Aimee tailored her instruction to match Simone's needs, increase her abilities, and meet her goals. Together she and Simone learned to achieve excellence.

TRY, TRY AGAIN

Practicing the familiar routines of Levels 1 through 6 over and over, step by step, builds a necessary baseline of confidence and ability. Gymnasts experience the added pressures of competition while they are being tested to perform their best.

Level 7 brings a more complex set of challenges for JO gymnasts. The degree of difficulty of required skills increases, and so does the pressure that comes with stepping up to the state and regional levels. Simone was eager to push forward, but she may have taken on too much, too quickly. She added new moves and combinations to her skill set, but she stumbled—literally—when she got to the Level 7 test. She was forced to repeat Level 7 before moving on.

Failing the Level 7 test the first time around was a difficult setback for Simone to process mentally and emotionally. However, it gave her a chance to think through exactly what she wanted from the sport and expected from herself. Simone was committed to winning. She needed to transform that goal into being committed 110% to excellence. Anything less wouldn't be enough.

Back at the gym, Simone worked to perfect and polish her skills. Setting up a practice regimen and sticking to it is one thing, but she soon realized that making the mental commitment is a separate step. Simone channeled her abilities and adjusted her attitude. She repeated moves, building muscle mass and muscle memory, until each part of every routine became second nature. Her dedication and determination paid off. When she entered the Level 7 competition for the second time, she was more than ready to succeed, and she did.

During 2007, Simone kept up her steady practice pace and mastered the skills necessary to get through Level 8 and Level 9. This meant overcoming her fears to execute more difficult connections on the uneven bars. Adria had recently returned to gymnastics, so Simone always had a gym buddy, and Aimee—who had never coached past Level 8—was learning right along with Simone as she improved and expanded her skill set. Once Simone achieved Level 9, Aimee knew that gymnastics would become a whole new ballgame. Girls who make it that far and keep going are aiming for an elite career. Simone was already spending several hours a day at the gym after school. But from here on out, everything about participating in the sport would get more demanding. Was Simone ready to make the sacrifices?

4

CHALLENGES AND CHOICES

By now, Simone was 11 years old and a sixth-grader. Though she was competing against girls who were older, taller, and more experienced, she just kept getting better, stronger, and more confident. She was having fun, and she was winning. As she got the attention of other coaches in a widening circle, Simone's parents began to take her ability more seriously.

A TURNING POINT

Up until this time, Ron and Nellie had supported Simone's interest without thinking too hard about her future in the sport. As long as she was happy and enjoying herself, that was all that mattered to them. Now they began to consider her talent and her triumphs and fully appreciate where the sport could take her. They went to Aimee for guidance and advice. Aimee felt that as long as the stress and pressure weren't getting in Simone's way, she should be allowed to compete as often as she wanted. Ron and Nellie agreed. Simone agreed, too. She was determined to become an elite-level gymnast and earn a spot on the national team. She didn't have any intention of stopping.

Simone also fantasized about the 2012 Olympics, still four years away, even though she knew there was a snag in her dreams: she was too young. To compete at the Olympics, you have to be 16 by the end of the Olympic year; Simone would not turn 16 until March 2013. If she wanted to be an Olympian, she was looking at *eight years* of training and competing before she would get her chance in 2016. How could she predict the way her life would unfold by the time she turned 19? Many gymnasts have gone as far as they can go in the sport when they hit their late teens, even if they stay strong and avoid injuries. Would she be able to stick with it that long?

One night, as Simone wrestled with all the unknowns that blocked her path to the future, she paused just long enough to see the one thing she really wanted. She wanted to go as far as she could. It was as simple as that. She recorded her thoughts in her diary and set her course.

FOUR-LEGGED INCENTIVE

When it comes to striving for tough goals, there is no such thing as too much motivation.

In spring 2008, Ron Biles was helping Simone fill out her paperwork for an upcoming and critical competition. She would need high scores in order to qualify for the Level 9 Western Championship. A lot depended on an ace performance. The top USAG officials would be there, including Martha Karolyi, the coordinator for the national team. Getting Martha's attention was key, and being invited to train with her was a big honor and a huge deal. But Simone and Adria had their hearts set on getting a dog, and this was uppermost in Simone's mind as her dad signed her up for this all-important meet.

THE KAROLYIS

Bela and Martha Karolyi first got attention on the world stage for coaching Romanian gymnast Nadia Comăneci. At the 1976 summer games in Montreal, Nadia was the first gymnast in Olympic history to score a perfect 10 (under the old scoring system). In 1981, the Karolyis defected from Romania and were granted political asylum by the United States.

The training system the Karolyis developed and perfected in Eastern Europe soon became the standard for USAG teams. From 1984 to 2016, it was impossible to pursue an elite career without being recognized by Martha or Bela Karolyi and attending camp at their ranch. In 2000, their facility, built on a huge spread near Huntsville, Texas, became the official USAG women's training center. Bela Karolyi stepped into the wings as Martha took over the program.

Though many athletes and coaches have a high regard for the Karolyis, some question their legacy. Both Bela and Martha Karolyi held a lot of power for a long time. Their program got proven results, but their methods for building physical and mental strength could be harsh. They demanded excellence and top performance. They may have fallen short when it came to providing security and protection.

Begging and pleading by Simone and Adria could not move Ron to agree to buy a dog, but he was willing to strike a bargain. If Simone did well enough to qualify for the Western Championship, Ron would get the family a German shepherd.

A pup named Maggie joined the family that summer after Simone's victory. (And three of Maggie's puppies followed later!)

2010

Simone blasted through Level 9. She was committed to becoming an elite gymnast and declared her intentions to her family. Everyone was glad to support her, but two things were posing problems. First, the family was getting ready to move—a move that meant leaving friends, changing schools, and adding a 45-minute commute between home and Bannon's. Second, to continue to the next levels, Simone would need to log more hours at the gym—more than the 20 hours a week she spent there already. Where would she find the time?

Nellie and Aimee arrived at a solution. Nellie enrolled Simone in a private school located across the street from the gym to finish out seventh grade and complete eighth grade. Simone trained from 7 A.M. to 9 A.M., went to school all day, and then returned to the gym for a second session. This increased her practice time to 30 hours a week.

It was, by any standard, a full schedule. Still, it might have worked out perfectly except for one big problem: Simone and the new school were not a good fit. At all. Simone struggled through, but she couldn't wait to be reunited with her friends when they all went to the same high school starting in ninth grade. In the meantime, she was glad to retreat to the friendly familiarity of the gym every day, and the extra time she was spending there began to make a real difference.

Up until the Level 9 and 10 competitions, more attention is paid to team scores than individual wins. At Level 10, USAG starts to identify the cream of the crop, tracking the gymnasts that might be chosen for assignments on the national and international stage.

Simone logged her first Level 10 win at the Houston National Invitational in 2010. There were 652 competitors, and Simone finished first on the vault, first on the floor exercise, and third in the all-around. Aimee followed up this achievement by applying to Martha Karolyi's developmental camp on Simone's behalf. But Martha chose not to ask Simone to attend. She didn't think Simone was ready for high-stakes competition—and didn't necessarily think she ever would be.

When Martha Karolyi turned Simone down, Nellie Biles, who had for years stayed on the sidelines as Simone pursued her interest in gymnastics, stepped in with uncharacteristic interference. Did Simone need a new coach at a different gym? No one at Bannon's had experience coaching at the elite levels of the sport. Nellie wasn't sure Aimee had the know-how to do the job. In the end, Aimee made Nellie a promise: she would continue to work with Simone, but she would seek advice and expertise from coaches at other gyms if she ever felt she couldn't provide the level of training Simone needed.

Simone was relieved that she could stick with Aimee. Aimee knew how to push Simone through her stubborn streaks and how to help her keep the stress level to a

Simone and Aimee

minimum. More than that, she had earned Simone's trust. Aimee was someone that Simone had come to rely on without question as both a mentor and friend— an important connection that would be hard to establish with a new coach.

Simone once again redoubled her efforts and focused her energy to perfect her skills. Aimee prepared Simone hour by hour. At the gym, she had Simone practice routines that were more and more demanding; at meets, she encouraged Simone to have fun and do her best. Their work together got the desired results: Simone qualified for the JO national competition that was held in Dallas. She placed first on the floor and third in the all-around, and she wrapped up the season as the 2010 U.S. Challenge Pre-Elite All-Around Champion. An invitation to Karolyi Ranch was all but certain.

MOVING UP

Simone spent time studying her sport when she wasn't practicing it. She was fascinated by the successful elite gymnasts, tumbling their way from city to city all around the world. She looked to their life stories for inspiration and their athletic journeys for guidance. What did she need to do to excel at that heady level? She needed to develop skills with a higher degree of difficulty.

Early in 2011, Simone tried out some of her high-scoring routines at the Gliders National Elite Qualifier. This was Simone's debut on the junior elite stage, a perfect storm of twitchy energy and pure concentration. As she moved from apparatus to apparatus, she was super aware—and super critical—of every wobble and step. But at the end of the day, she was number one in the vault and the all-around champion. Her high scores earned her a spot at the American Classic competition held at Karolyi Ranch, where all her next steps would be decided: competing at the Visa National Championships and being chosen for the junior national team. Simone had been training for eight years; the next four months could decide everything.

ADHD

As focused as Simone could be at the gym—analyzing every move, making a million subtle adjustments, following a strict practice regimen—she struggled to pay attention in school. The slightest distraction interrupted her train of thought, and it was difficult for her to stay on task. Toward the end of the school year, Ron

Biles had Simone tested for ADHD. No one was surprised when the diagnosis was confirmed. Simone's over-the-top energy wasn't exactly a secret. She had been a turbocharged toddler, and it was her extra spark and spirit that had inspired Nellie Biles to enroll Simone in gymnastics in the first place. Simone could blow off a lot of steam at the gym. Medication helped her when she needed to slow down and sit still.

During the 2016 Olympic Games, Simone's prescribed use of Ritalin was leaked to the press by hackers in an effort to throw shade on her achievements. Simone fired back in a tweet: "I have ADHD and I have taken medicine for it since I was a kid. Please know, I believe in clean sport, have always followed the rules, and will continue to do so as fair play is critical to sport and is very important to me."

Simone knows that having ADHD is nothing to be ashamed of, and she isn't afraid to let people know that she takes the medication she needs. In fact, any number of exceptional athletes live with ADHD, including Michael Phelps, Michael Jordan, Serena Williams, Nicole Vaidišová, Shane Victorino, and Carl Lewis.

Simone's scores at Gliders finally got her an invitation to attend a training camp at Karolyi Ranch in preparation for the American Classic. Martha Karolyi might have believed 14-year-old Simone was past her prime, but she was willing to give her a chance anyway. Simone was excited by the news. Maybe she would get to meet some of the athletes from the national team whom she idolized. And didn't the whole idea of camp sound like fun?

KAROLYI RANCH

The Karolyis can take credit for a long line of Olympic champions. For years, they hand-picked members of the national team and groomed them for greatness. Athletes attended five-day developmental camps every four to six weeks for intense training and testing. The 2,000-acre Karolyi Ranch could host up to 300 athletes and coaches at a time.

The idea of camp does sound like fun, but Karolyi Ranch was not *that* kind of camp. Thoughts of s'mores and stories around the campfire were quickly replaced by the reality of eight-hour practice days designed to get results. This was no-nonsense, hard-driving skill drilling meant to push each athlete past her limits. Martha Karolyi demanded nothing short of perfection. Any athlete who didn't share that goal was in the wrong place.

At first, Simone *did* feel that she was in the wrong place. The strict and rigid style of coaching at the ranch didn't suit her personality or her temperament. At Bannon's, Simone relied on good humor, chatting, jokes, and plenty of giggling to help keep from getting too wound up. At camp, Martha demanded no-nonsense behavior and a poker-faced demeanor to reflect a serious attitude toward the sport. Luckily, Aimee was at Simone's side to offer support and help keep her focused. And Simone knew that she just had to push herself, no matter what. Being invited to the ranch was a rite of passage, and being allowed to train there was a privilege. Simone had to show that she deserved to be there, and she had to dig deep to do it. The Karolyis' training method was not what Simone preferred, but it was what would get her the results she needed to up her game. She wouldn't reach the next level any other way.

Simone's cooperation and hard work proved successful a few weeks later. She returned to Karolyi Ranch for the American Classic competition. Her third-place win in the all-around was more than enough for her to qualify for the CoverGirl Classic and the Visa National Championships.

DISAPPOINTMENT AND DECISIONS

In the training sessions back at Bannon's leading up to the CoverGirl Classic, Simone continued to struggle on the uneven bars. She had spent nearly a year trying to perfect a complicated catch-and-release move (called a Tkatchev)—one that she needed to take to Nationals. Fall after fall made the move unnerving and scary, but Simone was determined to master it. She wanted to prove to

Gymnasts must overcome the fear factor to tackle the Tkatchev.

herself that she could overcome her fear and increase her skill set. She also didn't want to make a fool of herself on the national stage.

By the time she got to the CoverGirl meet, Simone's stress level was through the roof. She retreated to the restroom to hide her tears and try to gather her wits before her bar routine and was lucky enough to bump into Lexie Priessman, another competitor in her group. Lexie got Simone to pull herself together and gave her an inside tip on how to perform the Tkatchev perfectly every time by tweaking her timing. And it worked! Simone fell

Simone competing at Visa National Championships in St. Paul, MN, 2011

off the bars on two other parts of her routine, but she nailed the Tkatchev—another rung in her climb up through the ranks.

At the U.S. National Championships a few weeks later, Simone's performance was good but not good enough. She missed making the national team by just one spot, and it would be a year before she got another chance. Simone congratulated the other girls and bravely kept a smile on her face until she got back to the hotel with her family. Then she lost it. *Almost* making the junior women's team was not what she had trained so hard for, and she couldn't stop crying.

The emotions Simone was feeling were compounded by the expectations she had put on herself. She had not yet fully mastered the art of moving through defeats, which can hinder progress and play with your head. And she was carrying the burden of feeling as if she'd let everyone down.

An over-the-phone pep talk from her brother Ron

helped put Simone back on track. Almost making the team provided inspiration when Simone got back to work at Bannon's. Ron assured Simone that her day would come. And in the meantime, she needed to be kinder to herself. Simone took Ron's words to heart.

When Simone and Aimee got a chance to analyze the video of Simone's performance, one omission stood out: Simone hadn't included a move on the vault that Martha Karolyi had specifically wanted to see. It would have pushed the difficulty level up a notch, and the extra points might have made the difference. But more difficult often means more dangerous. Simone couldn't help but question her decision. In the end, however, she knew she had done the right thing. Simone had opted against including the skill not because it was scary but because she wasn't prepared. Performing it wouldn't have been safe. It hadn't been worth the risk.

Simone did feel the sting of defeat, but her failure— or what she came to realize was her lack of success—just made her want to work harder. Aimee was sure that more practice would get results. If Simone could be completely confident in her every move at the gym, she wouldn't let nerves get the better of her in competition. All good. The only problem was finding the extra time the extra effort would require.

Up until this moment, Simone had been dreaming of doing and having it all—elite gymnastics and a full schedule of classes and activities at school, including clubs, games, friends, and dates. High school was about to begin, and she couldn't wait. She'd be reunited with her friends from her old neighborhood, and they'd been making plans for months. Simone knew that she had to give up certain things in order to keep up her training schedule and allow time for travel to competitions. But she didn't want to give up going to high school.

It soon became clear, though, that Simone would have to make a choice, and she had a hard time weighing her options. The process wasn't easy for her family, either, as night after night they discussed the possibilities. Simone wanted to find a compromise, but for her parents it was an either/or decision. It was fine with them if she decided to go to high school and enjoy every single minute of it, but doing so would mean giving up her dream of being on the national team. She wouldn't have to give up gymnastics entirely; she could keep up her training and then compete when she got to college. But would that be enough?

Even as Simone argued with her parents, she knew that homeschooling was really the only answer. She also knew that her talent for gymnastics was a very special gift. She had a unique chance to excel in a sport she loved. She shouldn't waste that opportunity.

The decision to be homeschooled was painful, but it was the right thing to do. And it paid off. At the Visa National Championships in 2012, Simone made the junior national team.

5

THE WORLD STAGE

For Simone, competing on the national team seemed like plenty to focus on for the time being, but it was hard for her to watch the 2012 Summer Olympic Games in London without getting ahead of herself. It was thrilling to see the American gymnasts—called the Fierce Five—take first place. Simone had been to training camps at Karolyi Ranch with girls on that winning team. Could she really be on the podium in 2016?

• • •

THE FIERCE FIVE

The team the United States sent to the 2012 Olympics in London— Gabby Douglas, McKayla Maroney, Aly Raisman, Kyla Ross, and Jordyn Wieber—was at the time said to be the strongest in history, and the women exceeded all expectations. They easily earned the first-place slot in the qualifying round and took home the gold with a staggering five-point edge over the second-place Russian team. In a surprise upset, Aly Raisman and Gabby Douglas advanced to the all-around final ahead of their teammate and reigning champion, Jordyn Wieber; Gabby went on to win history-making gold.

The 2012 Fierce Five on the podium at the London games: Left to right: Jordyn Wieber, Gabrielle Douglas, McKayla Maroney, Alexandra Raisman, and Kyla Ross.

In January 2013, two slots opened up on the American Cup team, and Martha Karolyi chose Simone and Katelyn Ohashi to join the squad. This would be Simone's first chance to compete at such a high level—and her first experience dealing with the increased publicity, press, fans, and television coverage.

As the competition got underway, Simone was suffering from major jitters. It wouldn't take much to feel overwhelmed. It was hard enough for her to keep her nerves in check, let alone to cope with the added pressure of wanting to please Martha Karolyi. Still, she was doing fine until she crashed over the side of the balance

Simone at 2013 American Cup

beam on a back handspring. She became so flustered and worried about what Martha would say that she almost missed her remount—an athlete has only 30 seconds to get back on an apparatus after a fall in order to continue her routine. At the end of the meet, Simone was surprised and relieved when Martha congratulated her. For a first assignment at a higher level of competition, Simone had done well. But Martha's compliments didn't come without a caution. She let Simone know that getting into shape mentally would be just as critical as being in shape physically to meet the demands of high-stakes competition.

HIGHS AND LOWS

As Simone turned 16, she was in good spirits. She had cruised through her international competitions beside her idols—who were now her teammates. In Italy and Germany, she racked up big wins for herself and for her team.

Home again at Bannon's, Simone couldn't focus and had trouble getting back into a serious practice routine, but she also didn't seem to think she needed to. Aimee warned Simone repeatedly that she had to keep pushing herself to train harder. Aimee could see that Simone was taking her winning streak for granted—but not for long.

The Secret U.S. Classic was held in Chicago in July 2013. The competition was barely under way when Simone began to feel the effects of having slacked off at the gym. On the uneven bars, she missed the catch on the Tkatchev, something that hadn't happened in a couple of years. She would need to nail all of her other events to make up for the fall. Rattled and distracted, she tottered through her routine on the beam, missing every connection. By the time she got to the floor exercise, her tired legs felt like rubber, and she knew this was because she hadn't spent enough time preparing. She got off to a good start, but ran out of steam on the final tumbling pass. She couldn't make her last rotation and pitched forward on the landing; she tweaked an ankle and almost smashed her face into the mat. At that point, Aimee pulled her from the competition. Simone protested, but she knew Aimee was right. Mental mistakes can lead to physical catastrophe even if you are performing at 100%, and Simone was nowhere close to that. Later, Martha put the blame squarely in Simone's corner. Preparation meant focus and training; Simone lacked both.

THE TURNAROUND

Back at the gym, Simone had less than a month to get ready for Nationals, and she had work to do. Her mantra was "better, stronger, more consistent" as she went over and over each skill. In addition, she had a private coaching session with Martha at the ranch. Martha told her to own her talent and ignore the outside expectations that come with excellence. She should be in it for herself. No one and nothing else mattered. Simone took Martha's advice to heart.

Simone's sports psychologist, Robert Andrews, agreed. Simone met with him, hoping to relieve some of the pressure she was feeling. Andrews specializes in working with athletes whose level of training and ambition does not leave room for weakness of any kind. It can be hard for these top perform-ers to admit that they struggle with frayed nerves and buck-ling anxiety while they aim for the perfection required by their coaches and demanded by their fans. Andrews helps his clients overcome obsta-cles and keep expectations in check. He reminded Simone that she did her best when she went out onto the floor and just had fun. Simone needed to get back to that place where flying

In the zone and unbeatable

through the air was pure joy, without worrying about anything or anyone else.

Simone took her hard work and new attitude to the 2013 P&G National Championships. She won silver in all four events and won gold in the all-around. At the end of the meet, she had earned a place on the U.S. national senior team. A few weeks later, Martha Karolyi selected Simone to join the U.S. World Championship team. She would travel to Belgium in September with McKayla Maroney, Kyla Ross, and Brenna Dowell to compete for the title of best artistic gymnast in the world.

"It's amazing to get a second gold medal," said Biles. "It is such an honor to represent the United States. We came here to do a job, and we did it!"

WORLDS IN ANTWERP

Simone's performance at the World Championships in Antwerp, Belgium, in September and October 2013 marked a new level in her approach to competition and the results she could hope for. She moved through the competition neck and neck with teammate and friend Kyla Ross, the only member of London's 2012 Fierce Five to enter the competition. And at each event Simone glowed, letting her sense of delight shine through her performance. She became the first U.S. gymnast in over 20 years to qualify for the finals on all four apparatuses, and she captured gold in the all-around. For Simone, the key to success is going out there and having fun. And at Antwerp she was indeed having fun.

Included in her floor exercise at the Worlds was a new combination Simone had developed with Aimee while she was trying not to aggravate a strained calf muscle. She did her usual double layout, with her body as straight as a poker and fully extended for two full rotations in the air, and then added an extra half twist at the end. It meant executing a blind forward landing, meaning that Simone couldn't see the ground as she came down, but the impact was easier on her calves. Simone added the combination to the second tumbling pass of her floor routine, a high-stakes move. According to the rules, if she executed the new skill successfully in the competition, it would be named after her.

Since 2013, many gymnasts have added the Biles to their practice schedule or their floor routine.

She rocked it.

Winning the all-around finals made Simone the 2013 Artistic Gymnastics World Champion and the first African-American to win the title. After her disappointment at not making the national team in 2011, Simone's brother Ron had consoled her, insisting that her day would come. At the time, she might not have believed him, but she had been grateful for his belief in her. But now Ron's words rang with a special, crystal-clear truth; and when he told Simone to keep dreaming, she paid attention.

Simone hasn't lost a meet since.

6

DREAMING AND DREAMING BIG

Early in February 2014, Aimee Boorman walked out of Bannon's in the middle of practice. Simone and Adria felt a sense of helplessness and confusion as they watched her go. The tension that had been building for a while between Aimee and other employees at the gym had finally caused a permanent rift. But regardless of the upheaval, uncertainty, and inconvenience, Simone and Adria wanted to continue working with Aimee. There was no question that wherever she went, they would go, too. But where would that be?

WCC

In searching for answers, Nellie Biles spoke with Aimee and came up with a surefire plan for the athletes in the Biles household: she and Ron would build their own gym.

Within a week, they had purchased property near their home in Spring. Nellie was a partner in a chain of nursing homes that was already up for sale. Proceeds could be used to finance the creation of a new training center.

With determination, purpose, dedication, and care, Nellie and Ron Biles put their venture in motion. Building the World Champions Centre (WCC) would take a couple of years, so in the meantime Ron and Nellie leased space—first at a local gym and later at a warehouse they outfitted themselves—so that Aimee could continue coaching the girls.

Even though Aimee and Simone's parents quickly and sensibly found a way for her to keep up her training, the hasty exit from Bannon's and the changes that came with it were hard on Simone. She injured her shoulder at camp and was unable to participate in the first half of the 2014 competition season. She worked on healing in physical therapy sessions and went to the temporary gym every day, but she couldn't train properly for six months.

WIN GOLD, REPEAT

Being sidelined was difficult for Simone, and reentry was bumpy, too. Aimee's duties were spread thin as she oversaw the coaching for a growing group of gymnasts and worked to get WCC established so that it would be up and running when the construction was complete. Simone felt neglected without Aimee's guidance and care. Simone broke down as she finally expressed her anger and frustration, and Aimee broke down as she acknowledged Simone's pain. Simone then refocused her efforts and returned to her training routine—what she often refers to as persuading yourself, again and again, that you probably won't die even though you feel as though you will—and Aimee committed the time to refocus her efforts as Simone's main coach. In August, Aimee traveled with Simone to the P&G National Championships in Pittsburgh, and was the first to congratulate Simone on becoming U.S. champion for the second time.

Simone again made the national team and was chosen to go to Nanning, China, to compete at the World Championships in October 2014. Simone was excited to repeat this opportunity, but she was nervous, too. The first World Championships following an Olympic year do not include a team competition. Olympic competitors often retire or take time off after the games, so many countries cannot put together a full team. The 2013 World Championships in Belgium had not included the pressure of the team competition; the 2014 World Championships in China would include both the individual and team competitions. Simone recognized that any mistakes would not only put her own performance at risk, they would affect the combined score for her teammates, too.

As it turned out, Simone's conscientious and concerted effort plus her spectacular skills helped Team USA come out on top. Simone won gold on the beam and floor, and silver on the vault. She also received the all-around gold medal, even though she had downgraded the difficulty level on her uneven bar routine to protect her shoulder.

SIMONE CREATES A BUZZ

Standing on the podium to receive her gold medal as the all-around champion, Simone didn't notice the bee hiding among the blossoms of her bouquet. Silver medalist Larisa Lordache pointed to it, and Simone promptly freaked out! When she shook the bee free from her flowers, it went after her, chasing her off the podium.

Simone hopped behind the podium, ducking and dodging. She worried that the host nation was angry and worried that she was disgracing family, flag, and country. But mostly she worried about the bee. When the bee buzzed off to burrow into Kyla Ross's bouquet, Simone rejoined the other medalists, giggling on the podium. They all managed to get it together enough to show the proper decorum and pose for their picture as world champions.

The video of Simone and the bee went viral worldwide. It gave everyone a chance to get to know Simone's loopy, funny, playful, spontaneous, bee-fearing personality.

Everyone in the Biles family agreed that it had taken a lot of faith to get through the year of changes and challenges leading up to Simone's trip to China. Still, every step had provided insight, joy, resolve, and opportunity. Simone was grateful for the chance to do her best in the company of friends, and this bright, relaxed attitude rubbed off on everyone around her—even the stern, strict, and uncompromising Martha Karolyi.

MAKING HISTORY

When Simone traveled to Glasgow, Scotland, in 2015 for the World Championships, she was poised to make history. If she kept up her winning streak, she could become the only American to three-peat at Worlds, as well as the most decorated Worlds gymnast ever. No pressure!

Simone had learned from experience to put other people's expectations on a back burner and focus on her workouts. But the team had arrived in Glasgow early to overcome jet lag, and the daily workouts had been strenuous and exhausting. Simone began to overthink her every move and overanalyze a long list of what-ifs—an endless set of disastrous possibilities that were never a good idea to pursue. As a result, Simone was super keyed up when it came time to compete.

It was bad enough that her floor routine almost

got away from her and she landed out of bounds on an extra-energetic tumbling pass. On the balance beam, she let the crowd noise knock her off her game. As Simone went into a front tuck, the crowd responded enthusiastically to the British gymnast finishing up her floor routine nearby. Simone started to topple and grabbed the beam for dear life—a big error with a smaller deduction than an out-and-out fall.

THE ART OF IGNORING DISTRACTIONS

A gymnastics competition is like a three-ring circus—there are routines going on at every apparatus, with teams and coaches milling around, judges conferring, music blaring. Gymnasts learn to block out the hubbub around them. They try to time their starts to avoid or anticipate home-crowd interruptions. A break in concentration at the wrong time can obviously affect performance—and not in a good way.

Because her difficulty levels were so high and her deductions were minor, Simone was still able to blow past all her opponents, proof that after so much training, her routines were as automatic as breathing—or flipping through the air backward with a twist. The way Simone describes it is almost like an out-of-body experience. When asked about her win, Simone said she wished she could step out of herself while she was competing, to watch each dazzling move. And while some might not have been surprised that Simone came out ahead, she herself was shocked that she had pulled it off just the way she dreamed she would. She tried to find a way to process her success, but her immediate sense of elation was overcome by sheer exhaustion.

She was glad to get on a plane and return to Spring, where the World Champions Centre was about to hold its grand opening. The full measure and meaning of her achievement didn't hit Simone for another week. When it did, it brought her to her knees in a flood of emotion.

On the balance beam, Simone shows breathtaking grace and show-stopping skill.

GOING FOR GOLD

Schools with top **NCAA Division 1** gymnastics programs had been keeping an eye on Simone for years. Coaches had contacted her and had come to observe her at practices and at meets. Along with competing in the Olympics, joining a college gymnastics team had been Simone's long-time goal.

Simone's parents were impressed with the excellent program at the University of Alabama, and it had the advantage of being close to home. Even so, Simone had her heart set on heading west. A number of the elite gymnasts she knew from camp attended UCLA already, and Simone had a good rapport with the Bruins. A visit to UCLA convinced Simone that joining the Bruins squad was the best choice. Simone felt right at home, and finally—*finally*—she would be able to enjoy the normal social whirl of friends and dates and activities that she had given up as a homeschooler during high school.

By the time Simone got back to Spring after her visit to Los Angeles, her mind was made up. Over her parents' cautions and objections, Simone went ahead and committed to UCLA. She would start in the fall of 2015; if she made the Olympic team, she'd defer enrollment for a year. Simone was happy with her decision. It would be the perfect way for her to finish out her gymnastics career.

As so often is the case, Simone's choice was not as clear-cut as she wanted or expected it to be.

A GOLDEN OPPORTUNITY

Simone's success at the Worlds had opened her door to sports marketers and corporate sponsors. So far, she had resisted their offers. But going professional and going to the Olympics were a natural fit. Sponsors wanted to take advantage of the publicity buzz leading up to the Olympic Games. Simone could use her hard work and achievements to lock in financial security for the future. It was literally a golden opportunity. However, Simone knew full well that accepting money from sponsors would make her ineligible to compete for UCLA or any other college. In addition, Simone knew that time wasn't on her side. Unlike runners, swimmers, and soccer or volleyball players, gymnasts age out of their sport comparatively early. Most get only one chance to go to the Olympics. Barring an injury, competing in the upcoming 2016 Olympics was for Simone a sure thing. But going to college and then turning pro in the hopes of competing at the 2020 games? That was a very long shot.

Simone spent time weighing her options and bouncing them off of her family members. But it didn't matter what anyone else's opinions were or how much advice she got: she was the one who had to make the decision. In the end, Simone gave up her slot on the UCLA squad and got an agent instead.

Simone now had to keep an increasing list of sponsors happy along with the rest of her commitments and responsibilities. Still, she didn't forget for one moment that keeping herself happy was her main and most critical job. At the same time, she worked hard to prepare for each phase of the upcoming competition season, practicing new routines and adding new combinations. Martha Karolyi picked the elite assignments carefully. Martha wanted to maximize exposure without having her athletes burn out before the games in Rio, and she needed to protect them from injuries and wear and tear. Simone kept up her training schedule, and her agent helped squeeze in a new raft of duties and obligations.

RUN-UP TO THE OLYMPIC GAMES

In June, Simone turned in a shaky but still breathtaking performance at the National Championships. She won her fourth-straight all-around title, beating the field by nearly four points. Simone was proud of her win but more determined than ever to be her best, regardless of the score. The Olympic Trials would be her next test and her next chance to shine.

Even with all the hours and hours spent preparing at the gym, when Simone thought about going to the Olympics, she didn't think about competing at the games, she thought about just *being* at the games—representing the nation, tapping into the excitement, and sharing the unique experience with teammates and athletes from all over the world. What would it be like? Olympic veteran Aly Raisman told Simone that it was no different from any other international meet, and she should just plan to do what she had trained to do. Except, of course, it's the *Olympic Games!* Aly had two important tips: get lots of sleep, and don't look at the rings.

At the Olympic Trials, 14 women competed for five slots on the team. Eight of the 14 were world champi-

Making the 2016 Olympic team

ons, and two were returning Olympic champions. Simone placed first in the all-around with solid scores. Martha Karolyi named her to the team along with Aly Raisman, Gabby Douglas, Madison Kocian, and Laurie Hernandez; Ashton Locklear, MyKayla Skinner, and Ragan Smith were named as alternates. All the athletes had talents that added strength and depth to the team. Simone was on a high as the girls celebrated together.

But back at the WCC gym, Simone was having trouble with the uneven bars. She wasn't accustomed to the new, springier apparatus that matched what would be used in Rio, and she just couldn't get used to it. As she struggled physically to perfect her familiar routine, she struggled

Simone trained hard to get to Rio,
and she was ready.

8

RIO

Finally. The competition that Simone Biles had been waiting for and training for and preparing for and dreaming about for so many years: the 2016 Olympic Games in Rio de Janeiro.

Exhausted from the last practice push at camp, the team slept through the ten-hour flight from Houston to Rio. When they landed, they picked up speed. First up came publicity photos, check-in, traveling to the site, and getting settled before heading straight for their first practice at the gym.

The team was used to Martha's daily routine at the ranch, and it didn't let up once they got to Rio. They had morning and afternoon workouts on each apparatus, with a midday break. Practices were tiring, and the team was happy to retreat to their balcony to hang out and rest between workouts. Meanwhile, being in the Olympic Village was a huge thrill. Just walking around or eating in the cafeteria, the team was as starstruck as anyone when they met their idols.

COMPETING

Everyone on the American team did well at the qualification round. Simone, Aly, and Gabby finished in the top three positions, with the rest of the team close behind in the pack. All the girls on the team were more than qualified to meet the all-around challenge; but according to Olympic rules, only the top two finishers from each country would compete in the all-around.

Winning gold takes teamwork. Left to right: Aly Raisman, Madison Kocian, Laurie Hernandez, Simone, and Gabby Douglas.

On August 9, Team USA showed up to put all their hours and hours of training to the test. All of them performed with precision and poise, skill and grace. All of them contributed to the team's first-place win. And just like that, Simone was an Olympic gold medalist. She had reached her goal and exceeded her dreams, and she was only halfway finished with her Olympic experience. She needed to ride the crest through the all-around competition and event finals.

A GOOD DAY

The day of the all-around competition, Simone and Aly spent the morning alone together in the suite, curbing their excitement as they did their hair and makeup. They took the bus to the arena for their warm-up before the competition. Coming down to the wire, Simone's stomach began to do cartwheels. When she slumped onto a bench by the restroom, Aly was right beside her, pale and clammy. They sat there together, concentrating on their breathing to corral their nerves. They both had a job to do, and it was time to do it. Simone was glad to have an enthusiastic crowd as she and Aly entered the arena and got into the zone. Above the crowd noise, Simone listened for her mom's voice, cheering her on, assuring her that she had this in the bag.

Did she ever.

SKYROCKETING SCORE: 62.198

So much for the jinx. Simone became the first woman in 20 years to achieve back-to-back top spots in the all-around at both the Worlds and the Olympics. And Simone didn't just win the all-around; she crushed it. Simone scored two

Aly Raisman and Simone—fierce competitors and fast friends.

points higher than Aly, who won the silver—more than the difference between first and second place in the previous nine Olympic Games combined. In other words, every other gold medalist won by only fractions of a point. Simone won by a mile. (In the men's competition at Rio, Kōhei Uchimura of Japan beat out the silver medalist by 0.099 points.)

For the rest of the competition, the U.S. team continued to perform at the top of its game. In the individual events, Simone was the first American woman to win gold in the vault, something she hadn't been able to do in a world competition. A near fall and two-handed save on the beam cost her a full point and normally would have put her out of the medal race, but her level of difficulty was so high that she was still able to earn bronze behind her Olympic Village roommate, Laurie Hernandez. She skipped the uneven bars, leaving that job to Madison Kocian, who took silver. And when it came time for her floor exercise, Simone erupted with joy, enthusiasm, confidence, strength, beauty, mastery, and the power of flight. Gold all the way.

Celebrating with roommate and teammate, Laurie Hernandez.

2016 OLYMPIC MEDAL COUNT

RANKING	WOMEN'S INDIVIDUAL EVENTS
1 Gold	Simone Biles—All Around Simone Biles—Vault Simone Biles—Floor Exercise
2 Silver	Aly Raisman—All-Around Aly Raisman—Floor Exercise Madison Kocian—Uneven Bars Laurie Hernandez—Balance Beam
3 Bronze	Simone Biles—Balance Beam

Simone leading Team USA at the closing ceremony at Rio.

And among the highlights? Team USA chose Simone to be the flag-bearer at the ceremony to close the Rio games. President Barack Obama and First Lady Michelle Obama sent the following tweet:

Couldn't be prouder of #TeamUSA. Your determination and passion inspired so many of us. You carried that flag high tonight, @Simone_Biles!

Simone Biles. Quite possibly the Greatest of All Time.

9

STATS AND STANDINGS

When it comes to gymnastics, Simone has proved over and over again that she is in a class by herself. Even her weakest events can blow away the competition, and even her worst day can best the field.

Like other top athletes, Simone Biles stands out for her ability, discipline, performance, and accomplishments. But she also brings a special spark to her sport with her attitude. Simone would never have made it to the top tier of gymnastics if she hadn't been having fun along the way. She was lucky enough to find a coach who recognized her gifts but also understood her personality and pace. Aimee Boorman's philosophy and approach to coaching helped Simone fully explore her potential and get it onto the world stage.

Simone came home from Rio with four gold medals. Only four other gymnasts have earned this achievement at a single Olympics: Ágnes Keleti of Hungary and Larisa Latynina of the Soviet Union at the Melbourne games in 1956, Vera Caslavska of Czechoslovakia at the Mexico City games in 1968, and Ecaterina Szabo of Romania at the Los Angeles games in 1984.

Thanks to the astonishing point spread Simone racked up in the all-around, she helped put the U.S. into the record books. Simone was the fourth U.S. Olympian in a row to snag the gold medal. Carly Patterson won

Simone earned Olympic gold and her place in history.

at the Athens games in 2004, Nastia Liukin won at the Beijing games in 2008, and Gabby Douglas won at the London games in 2012.

Simone's medal count at the Olympics plus her 14 World Championship wins add up to a total of 19 medals so far, more than anyone else in USA Gymnastics history.

The following charts give an overview of Simone's career, beginning as a senior elite gymnast in 2013, and her personal best scores starting at Level 8.

* * *

SIMONE'S SCORES

DATE	MEET	VAULT	UNEVEN BARS	BEAM	FLOOR	ALL AROUND
7/24/13	2013 Secret U.S. Classic	0.000	13.650	13.950	13.700	41.300
7/31/14	2014 Secret U.S. Classic	15.900	14.750	15.250	15.800	61.700
8/18/14	2014 P&G National Championships	15.900	14.550	15.700	15.650	61.800
7/22/15	2015 Secret U.S. Classic	16.000	15.100	15.250	16.050	62.400
8/10/15	2015 P&G National Championships (Preliminaries)	16.250	15.150	14.800	14.900	61.100
8/10/15	2015 P&G National Championships	16.300	14.950	15.900	15.850	63.000
7/3/16	2016 Olympic Trials	16.000	14.950	15.200	15.700	61.850
Summer 2016	Olympic Games Qualification	16.000	15.000	15.633	15.733	62.366
Summer 2016	Olympic Games Final	15.866	14.966	15.433	15.933	62.198
2017 Did not compete						
7/28/18	U.S. Classic	15.400	13.350	15.200	14.750	58.700
8/18/18	U.S. Championships (Preliminaries)	15.600	14.850	15.200	14.450	60.100
8/19/18	U.S. Championships Final	15.600	14.550	14.900	14.700	59.750

SIMONE'S PERSONAL BESTS

LEVEL	VAULT	UNEVEN BARS	BEAM	FLOOR	ALL AROUND
8	9.500	8.900	9.000	9.150	36.500
9	9.370	8.750	8.700	9.375	36.200
10	9.825	9.325	9.600	9.850	38.050
Elite	12.850	9.350	12.050	12.450	46.700
Senior	16.300	15.150	15.900	16.050	63.000

10

CHASING BILES

The nature of gymnastics makes ongoing rivalries misleading on the one hand and short-lived on the other. Gymnasts competing as a team must work together to find the sweet spot, building on each other's strengths and supporting each other's efforts. As the saying goes, there is no *I* in *TEAM.* On the road, teammates who have spent countless hours practicing alone with their coaches travel, live, train, and compete together, building strong skills and strong connections. Everyone wants to win, and there are definitely people to beat, but a hundred combinations of flub and fluster can affect anyone's performance at any given time—tottery landings, slipped grips, shaky revolutions, and overextensions. Unpredictability keeps the standings as airborne as the tumblers.

A gymnast on top in one round can easily wobble out of contention in the next.

In addition, gymnastics is a revolving door in and out of adolescence. The time frame for competing is limited as athletes' bodies mature and change. Most gymnasts peak in their late teens, and many of the familiar names in U.S. gymnastics history retired by the time they were 20. Injuries force some competitors to hang up their leotards. Others who haven't gone pro take advantage of the opportunity to compete at the college level while they earn their degrees.

A NOTABLE EXCEPTION

Oksana Chusovitina is still competing at the age of 42 and fully intends to represent Uzbekistan at the Tokyo games in 2020—her eighth trip to the Olympics. At Rio, Chusovitina attempted the Produnova—a front handspring onto the vault and a double tucked somersault coming off of it— arguably the most difficult and dangerous skill in all of gymnastics. When Simone Biles was asked why she didn't try the Produnova, she responded by saying that she wasn't trying to die—and she wasn't really joking.

LEGENDS

A number of bright and daring pioneers have skills named after them, including Olga Korbut, Simona Amanar, Natalia Yurchenko, and Cheng Fei on the vault; Elise Ray, Nadia Comăneci, Dominique Dawes, and Betty Okino on the uneven bars; Kelly Garrison, Nastia Liukin, and Marisa Dick on the balance beam; and Oksana Chusovitina, Brandy Johnson, Brenna Dowell, and Simone Biles on the floor exercise. All these skills are described and quantified in the Code of Points, and all these names are familiar to gymnasts and fans.

LEADERS

As with any sport, only a fraction of those who participate go on to greatness. There are 3,000 women competing on college gymnastics teams across the country. All of them came to a crossroads as they moved past Level 7 and into the junior and senior elite levels, and all of them looked to their idols for insight and inspiration.

NADIA COMĂNECI (1961–)

Nadia Comăneci started training with Bela Karolyi in Romania in 1968 when she was seven years old. She was one of the first students at the gymnastics school run by Karolyi and his wife, Martha. Nadia competed across Europe, gaining recognition for her perfect scores (under the old 10-point scoring system). At the Montreal games in 1976, she was awarded the first perfect 10 in Olympic history for her routine on the uneven bars, and she went on to get six more 10s. She also won gold on the balance beam and the uneven

NADIA COMĂNECI

bars, silver for the team, and bronze for the floor exercise. An uneven bar dismount and salto are named for her.

At the 1980 games in Moscow—which were boycotted by the United States—Nadia won gold in the balance beam and the floor exercise. The following year, the Karolyis defected to the United States while wrapping up a "Nadia '81" tour. As a result, Nadia was not allowed to travel outside of Romania; authorities feared she would defect, too. She was granted permission to travel to the Los Angeles Olympics in 1984, but could not participate or contact the Karolyis. Nadia finally made the dangerous escape out of Romania in 1989. Gradually she made contact with old friends in the United States, including U.S. gymnast Bart Connors, whom she married in 1996.

MARY LOU RETTON

MARY LOU RETTON (1968–)

Mary Lou Retton captured the imagination of the nation and the world at the 1984 games in Los Angeles. She won the all-around competition, becoming the first American to win a gold medal in gymnastics. She went on to win four more medals—silver in team, silver in vault, and bronze in uneven bars and floor—more than any other athlete at the games that year.

SHANNON MILLER

SHANNON MILLER (1977–)

Shannon Miller was on top of the gymnastics scene during the 1990s and currently holds the career lead for Olympic wins. She won five medals at the 1992 games in Barcelona—bronze for the team medal, silver for the all-around (losing gold by the slimmest margin in Olympic history), silver on the balance beam, and bronze for the uneven bars and floor. She returned to the 1996 games in Atlanta to win team gold for the United States for the first time and was the first American gymnast to win gold on the balance beam.

NASTIA LIUKIN

NASTIA LIUKIN
(1989–)

Nastia Liukin—daughter of an Olympic gold-medal gymnast—took home five medals from the 2008 games in Beijing to tie with Mary Lou Retton and Shannon Miller for the most medals won at a single Olympics—gold in the all-around, silver in the team, silver on the uneven bars and the beam, bronze on the floor.

GABBY DOUGLAS

GABBY DOUGLAS
(1995-)

Gabby Douglas made history at the 2012 games in London as the first American gymnast to win gold in both the all-around and the team competitions at a single Olympics. She was also the first person of African descent from any nation to be the all-around champion. She repeated gold in the team competition at the 2016 Olympics in Rio as part of the Final Five.

Simone shows poise, a strong work ethic, and leadership both in and out of the gym.

11

BEYOND COMPARE

When you are trying to describe a standout athlete, it is hard to avoid making comparisons. Sports reporters and media commentators often feel a need to link an athlete's accomplishments to champions whose undisputed talents are widely known and loudly praised. The public has been duly dazzled by these superstars. Their remarkable skills set the bar at a dizzying height.

Simone's moves make history.

As a result, Simone's talent is often measured by others' achievements.

Simone Biles can propel herself so high into the air that she can execute two backflips and a twisting somersault with time to spare. Coming out of two back handsprings, she can launch herself six feet above a balance beam to execute two full rotations and a flip before she lands upright. Her ability to defy gravity makes her the Michael Jordan of women's elite gymnastics.

In the floor exercise, a burst of adrenaline can hurtle a gymnast right out of bounds. Simone has learned to control and contain her explosive power and use it to her advantage. She is the Usain Bolt of women's elite gymnastics.

Simone's discipline, determination, and fearless drive to test what's possible and then push past it have made her one of the most decorated gymnasts of all time. Simone is the Lindsey Vonn of women's elite gymnastics.

Since 2013, Simone has been on a winning streak of her very own. Any gymnast in a competition with Simone knows that silver is the one to beat; Simone, in a class by herself, is unbeatable. She is the Serena Williams of women's elite gymnastics.

These comparisons made in the press may be accurate, but they aren't necessary. Simone is not the Michael Jordan, Usain Bolt, Lindsey Vonn, or Serena Williams of women's elite gymnastics.

She is the one and only Simone Biles.

Next stop, 2020!

12

R&R — REST AND RETURN

After the Olympics in Rio, Simone took a year off. She needed a chance to rest—physically and mentally—recuperate, explore possibilities, and finally enjoy the normal everyday social life of a superstar. She may have been away from the gym, but this didn't mean she was off the road or off the grid. Speaking engagements, red-carpet events, and talk-show appearances kept her on the go.

Simone started a line of leotards that she designs herself. She signed on as spokesperson for a half dozen corporations. She became involved with Girls on the Run, helping girls build solid life skills and make healthy choices. She published an autobiography and consulted on a movie about her life. She started business classes at University of the People—an online, nonprofit college—and also serves as its global ambassador. She competed on *Dancing with the Stars* and marched into NRG stadium wearing bright red boots as an honorary cheerleader for the Houston Texans.

CHANGES

Apart from promotions and projects, Simone went on vacations with her family, moved into her own apartment, and got a boyfriend. She had fun and freedom for the first time in ages, and she made the most of both. Even so, gymnastics was always on her radar screen. After a year away, it was time to get back to the mats.

On November 1, 2017, Simone returned to the gym, more than ready to once again put her skills and determination to work. Experience proved to be both an asset and a curse: Simone knew what she needed to do to get results and understood the payoff. She also was well aware of the challenges, the risks, the physical demands, and the mental stamina that would be required. She reentered the gym with a seasoned outlook and a new coach to see her through.

After the Olympic Games in Rio, Aimee Boorman's career path took her to Florida. Simone might have followed her there, but the Biles family's investment, time, and energy were now devoted to making WCC a first-class training facility. Simone obviously has a huge stake in the success of WCC; moving away from Spring was not an option. After a thorough and thoughtful search, Laurent and Cecile Landi were hired to take over Simone's training.

COACH LANDI

When Simone found herself without a coach to guide her next steps, she chose Laurent Landi to head up her training. Landi is a former member of the French national team. He and his wife, Olympian-turned-coach Cecile Canqueteau-Landi, previously coached at the Bart Conner Gymnastics Academy in Norman, Oklahoma, and the World Olympic Gymnastics Academy in Texas before joining the Biles's staff at WCC. The couple has coached some of the top competitors in the sport, including Alyssa Baumann, Madison Kocian, and Katelyn Ohashi.

Simone has known Laurent and Cecile for a long time and appreciates their years of experience, shared expertise, and commitment to success. Coach Landi admires the tremendous accomplishments that Simone has already achieved. He does not plan to alter her style or her approach to the sport. He is willing to advise Simone as she determines a plan of action and then help her set it in motion.

THE COMEBACK

The press eagerly reported Simone's comeback, but she was reluctant to reveal long-term goals. She'd take it week by week, and then she and Coach Landi would set expectations accordingly. However, actions speak so much louder than words. Although Simone wouldn't make any predictions or promises as she resumed her work at the gym, her performance at the U.S. Classic in July 2018 was nothing short of dazzling.

Simone was back!

She was back in Columbus, Ohio, where her story began, being cheered on by her family. She was back in the groove, feeling the familiar surge of adrenalin, confidence, and joy. She was back on the podium to collect four more medals.

Simone was, of course, the first to point out the pitfalls and pick apart her record-busting performance: She bobbled her bar routine. She couldn't find her footing on her vault landing. She couldn't contain her power to stay in bounds on her floor exercise. Yet she managed to rack up the highest all-around score in the world since her dominance in Rio. Simone showed the world that she is capable of so much more than what she achieved at the Olympic Games. Even more importantly, she proved it to herself.

Part of the reason for this boost can be traced back to the limits Simone had to put on herself back in 2016. In the year leading up to the Olympics, Aimee felt that it was important for Simone to hit a level of excellence and hold fast, working on consistency without adding anything new. This approach obviously worked. Simone was able to get results that won gold. But with Rio in the record books, Simone was anxious to go back to pushing her limits, trying new moves, chipping away at challenges, and expanding her abilities.

Instead of imposing limits, Simone is now intent on pushing them just as far as they will go by increasing her range and improving her skill set. The Landis have presented Simone with new challenges that coax her out of her comfort zone and keep her interested. They mingle drills with silliness to keep Simone loose and light. They help Simone set small goals that have quickly started adding up to huge gains. A case in point: Simone can now blow away the field in what was once her weakest event—the uneven bars—thanks to inspired coaching and a new attitude.

Simone's three-point win at the U.S. Classic served as a handy reminder: It is safe to say that the only athlete who can beat Simone is Simone herself. No other competitor comes close to taking the top spot—and short of a catastrophe, that isn't going to change until Simone retires. Just in case there was any doubt, Simone proved the point at the 2018 U.S. Championships in Boston. She became the first woman in 24 years to sweep every event and the first to win the title five times. She also ended the two-day competition a whopping 6.5 points ahead of 2017 world champion Morgan Hurd; only .55 of a point separated Morgan from third-place finisher Riley McCusker.

Keep in mind that what Simone brings to the spotlight is only a glimpse of what she is practicing at the gym. Just when you think you've seen it all, there is much more to come.

THE FUTURE FOUR

A rules change means that a team of only four athletes will qualify for the 2020 Olympic Games in Tokyo. And though none of the Final Five have announced their retirement, Laurie Hernandez is the only one who has said that she might return to competition in 2019. Rio alternates Ashton Locklear and Ragan Smith cannot be ruled out. They made strong showings in 2017 but are currently battling injuries.

In addition to the veterans, talented contenders are working their way up the rankings, adding points to the difficulty of their routines and consistency to their executions. Besides Morgan Hurd and Riley McCusker, athletes making a strong showing for the U.S. at the Worlds were Kara Eaker and Grace McCallum. Others on the watch list include Jade Carey, Shilese Jones, and Trinity Thomas—all members of the 2018–2019 national team—as well as Jordan Chiles, who finished just out of the running. Some of these women are new to the senior elite stage, and Simone is glad to be able to mentor them as they gain experience.

THE WORLDS

The 2018 World Gymnastics Championships in Doha, Qatar, marked Simone's return to the world stage.

She made a somewhat shaky entrance.

A kidney stone landed Simone in the hospital the day before competition began. She had been experiencing pain for a couple of days before she left the United States. When her discomfort kept getting worse, Simone's parents persuaded her to go to the emergency room. Once she got the diagnosis, Simone opted to power on through. Doing so meant adding pain and lack of sleep to the usual obstacles and risks of any competition, including simply having an off day.

KIDNEY STONES

Kidney stones are mineral deposits that can form in your kidneys. Small stones can pass through your system, but they can cause major discomfort as they move around. In many cases, pain relief is the main treatment, along with lots of water, but doping rules prevented Simone from taking any medication.

In spite of being somewhat less than 100%, Simone got up the next morning ready to begin the competition. The women's team had won every Olympic and world team title since 2011. Simone was determined to do her part to keep the winning streak alive. Thanks to Simone's determination, the United States took first place and landed a spot at the 2020 Olympic Games. What's more, the margin of victory was 8.7666 record-breaking points ahead of second-place China.

Once again, bobbles and missteps chipped away at Simone's execution scores, but once again she was able to overcome them to add to her medal count. Simone's combinations, connections, and complicated dismounts put her ahead of the field by almost three points. Over the weeklong competition, Simone became the first American ever to medal in every event, adding six more medals to her impressive collection: gold medals in the team, vault, floor, and all-around events; a silver medal on the uneven bars; and a bronze medal on the beam. Simone arrived in Doha with a bad side ache and the exacting expectations she always puts on herself. She left Doha as the most decorated woman gymnast in world championship history.

THE G.O.A.T.

Simone Biles was born with an exceptional talent that set her on a unique path from her first hop onto the mat. With help, guidance, and love, she nurtured that ability and turned it into a phenomenon. She is stubborn, cheerful, spirited, and giving. Her empathy makes her kind, and her courage makes her one of a kind.

Simone has already reached and exceeded every benchmark needed to be declared the G.O.A.T., but she isn't yet finished with her trailblazing gymnastics career. After treatment for the kidney stone and a short vacation, Simone will return to the gym to train for competitions in 2019 that will decide the Olympic team. Tokyo 2020 is just around the corner. Whatever Simone takes on, you can be sure that she will continue to build the confidence she needs to test herself and best herself. You'll find her in the gym, dreaming of her next brilliant and breathtaking move.

GLOSSARY

AERIAL MOVES: Stunts in which the gymnast makes a complete turn in the air without touching the apparatus.

APPARATUS: A piece of equipment used in a gymnastics competition.

BALANCE BEAM: Beam apparatus that is about 4" wide, 16' long, and 4' off the ground for acrobatic and dance moves and a dismount.

DISMOUNT: To leave the apparatus at the end of a routine, and the skill used to do it.

ELITE: The highest level in gymnastics.

EXTENDED/EXTENSION: The height and stretch of raised arms during a dance move.

FLOOR: A 40' × 40' foam-covered spring floor for dance, tumbling, and acrobatic routine.

JO: Junior Olympics.

LAYOUT: A stretched-out body position, toes pointed, legs straight.

MOUNT: Getting onto an apparatus, and the skill used to do it.

NCAA DIVISION 1: The highest level of college athletics; National Collegiate Athletics Association.

SALTO: A flip or somersault; the feet come over the head and the body rotates around the axis of the waist.

SPRINGBOARD: Equipment required in the vault to reach the vaulting table.

TUCK: Knees and hips bent and drawn in to the chest, with the body folded at the waist.

UNEVEN BARS: Two parallel bars set at different heights: one is at 8' off the ground, and the other is 5'4" off the ground. They are set 6' apart for swinging skills, release moves, moving from one bar to the other, circling skills, and the dismount.

USAG: USA Gymnastics.

VAULT: A table that is 4' off the ground; the gymnast runs down the runway, springs off the springboard, pushes off the table, and lands on the floor beyond the table.

BIBLIOGRAPHY

Ahmed, Murad. "Simone Biles: A Gymnast Vaulting into Record Books." *Financial Times*, August 12, 2016. https://www.ft.com/content/df44e77c-5fd5-11e6-ae3f-77baadeb1c93.

"Anatomy of a Gymnast," February 26, 2017. youtube.com/watch?v-ycMPXvq5Ejw.73Questions.

"An Introduction to the Basic Moves on the Balance Beam in Gymnastics." SportsAspire, February 16, 2018. sportsaspire.com/gymnastics-balance-beam.

Aragon, Rose-Ann. "Simone Biles to Hold International Invitational at Family's World Champions Centre in Spring." KPRC, February 23, 2018. click2houston.com/news/simone-biles-to-hold-international-invitational-at-familys-world-champions-centre-in-spring.

Axon, Rachel. "Simone Biles Wins Third All-Around Title at World Gymnastics Championships." USA TODAY, January 22, 2019. usatoday.com/story/sports/olympics/2015/10/29/simon-biles-world-gymnastics-championships-all-around/74825328.

Bastién, Angelica Jade. "Why Historic Wins by Simone Biles, Simone Manuel Matter for Race in America." *Rolling Stone*, June 25, 2018. rollingstone.com/sports/simone-biles-and-simone-manuel-wins-impact-on-race-w434453.

Biles, Simone, with Burford, Michelle. *Courage to Soar*. Zondervan, 2016.

Biles, Simone. "Simone Biles." Biography, n.d. biography.com/people/simone-biles-051816.

Biles, Simone, and Roenigk, Alyssa. "Simone Biles on Her Return to Gymnastics, New Coach and New Partnership." EspnW, October 26, 2018. espn.com/espnw/life-style/article/21170158/simone-biles-return-gymnastics-new-coach-new-partnership.

Clarke, Liz. "Simone Biles Soars to Gymnastics All-Around Gold; Aly Raisman Takes Silver." Chicagotribune.com, August 11, 2016. chicagotribune.com/sports/international/ct-womens-gymnastics-all-around-rio-olympics-20160811-story.html.

"Code of Points|Balance Beam Gymnastics Skills." Code of Points, January 23, 2019. codeofpoints.com/balance-beam/.

Crawford, Aimee. "Bravo, Simone Biles, for Taking a Stand against ADHD Stigma." EspnW, September 21, 2018. espn.com/espnw/voices/article/17602540/bravo-simone-biles-taking-stand-adhd-stigma.

Davis III, Ossie. "Simone Biles: The Golden Girl—The Cincinnati Herald." *The Cincinnati Herald*, January 5, 2018. thecincinnatiherald.com/2018/01/simone-biles-golden-girl/.

Davis, Rachaell. "13 Black Women Who Changed the Face of Gymnastics." *Essence,* July 18, 2016. essence.com/celebrity/13-black-women-who-changed-face-gymnastics/.

"Earth-Shatteringly Amazing Facts and Objectives of Gymnastics." SportsAspire, February 19, 2018. sportsaspire.com/facts-objectives-of-gymnastics.

"Frame by Frame, Moves That Made Simone Biles Unbeatable." *The New York Times*, October 17, 2016. nytimes.com/interactive/2016/08/11/sports/olympics/simone-biles-winning-moves.html.

Graves, Will. "Olympic Champion Simone Biles Returns to Gym with New Coach." AP NEWS, October 17, 2017. apnews.com/9ea2a35ec5ca4fed99f-bc05e5941a03f.

"Gymnastics Levels Guide." Gymnastics HQ, October 27, 2011. gymnasticshq.com/gymnastics-levels/.

"Gymnastics Skills List: Floor." GymnasticsHQ, June 16, 2015. gymnasticshq.com/gymnastics-skills-list-floor.

Gymnastics, USA. "Simone Biles." Team USA, December 22, 2015. teamusa .org/usa-gymnastics/athletes/simone-biles.

Haden, Jeff. "Simone Biles and the 'Biles': How to Turn a Weakness into Innovation and Excellence." Inc.Com, May 17, 2018. inc.com/jeff-haden/ simone-biles-and-the-biles-how-to-turn-a-weakness-into-innovation- and-excellence.html.

Harrell, Roger J. "Definition of Gymnastics Terms:" drillsandskills.com/ definitions.

"Home—Mary Lou Retton." Mary Lou Retton, December 31, 2018. marylouretton.com/#bio.

Kiszla, Mark. "Kiszla: Sorry, Michael Phelps and Usain Bolt. Simone Biles Is the Best Olympian in Rio." *The Denver Post*, August 17, 2016. denverpost. com/2016/08/16/kiszla-sorry-michael-phelps-and-usain-bolt-simone- biles-wins-gold-as-best-olympian-in-rio/.

Kyle, Marni. "List of Gymnastics Beam Moves | Livestrong.Com." LIVESTRONG.COM, n.d. livestrong.com/article/417300-list-of- gymnastics-beam-moves/.

Leshovsky, Heather. "Understanding Women's Gymnastics Scoring|Emeth Gymnastics." Emeth Gymnastics, November 8, 2016. emethgym.com/team/ team-parent-resources/understanding-womens-gymnastics-scoring/.

Liu, Junhua. "USA Gymnastics Online: Athlete Shannon Miller," n.d. usagym .org/pages/athletes/archivedbios/m/smiller.html.

Lutz, Rachel, and Associated Press. "Simone Biles Wins First Meet since Rio Olympics with Fall." OlympicTalk, July 29, 2018. olympics.nbcsports. com/2018/07/28/simone-biles-wins-comeback-gymnastics-us-classic/.

Manning, Charles. "9 Fascinating Facts about Team USA's Sparkly Leotards." *Cosmopolitan,* October 9, 2017. cosmopolitan.com/style-beauty/fashion/a62586/olympic-leotard-facts/.

"Mastering the Kip in Gymnastics." SportsAspire, n.d. sportsaspire.com/mastering-kip-in-gymnastics.

McCarthy, Brigid. "40 Years Ago, Soviet Gymnast Olga Korbut Dazzled the World." Public Radio International, July 24, 2012. https://www.pri.org/stories/2012-07-24/40-years-ago-soviet-gymnast-olga-korbut-dazzled-world.

Megas, Natalia. "Upcoming Movie about Simone Biles Shows a Different Side of the Olympic Gymnast—The Lily." https://Thelily.Com, January 23, 2018. thelily.com/upcoming-movie-about-simone-biles-shows-a-different-side-of-the-olympic-gymnast/.

Meyers, Dvora. "Simone Biles Doesn't Want To Be A Savior." Deadspin, August 17, 2018. deadspin.com/simone-biles-doesnt-want-to-be-a-savior-1828415172.

Ochs, Carol. "Gymnastics Levels for Girls." How to Adult, n.d. howtoadult.com/144528-gymnastics-levels-for-girls.html.

Pang, Becca. "Simone Biles Returns to Gymnastics Training with New Coach Laurent Landi," n.d. flogymnastics.com/articles/6019897-simone-biles-returns-to-gymnastics-training-with-new-coach-laurent-landi.

Payne, Marissa. "'Vault of Death' Gymnast Scoffs at Retirement at Age 41." *The Washington Post,* May 23, 2017. https://www.washingtonpost.com/news/early-lead/wp/2017/05/23/vault-of-death-gymnast-scoffs-at-retirement-at-age-41/?utm_term=.11968652de42.

Phillips, Anne. "Simone Biles Becoming a Balanced All-Around Gymnast," n.d. flogymnastics.com/articles/5047015-simone-biles-becoming-a-balanced-all-around-gymnast.

Powers, John. "Simone Biles Wins Gold, Aly Raisman Silver in Individual All-Around Olympic Gymnastics." *The Boston Globe.* BostonGlobe.Com, n.d. bostonglobe.com/sports/olympics2016/2016/08/11/simone-biles-wins-gold-aly-raisman-silver-individual-all-round-olympic-gymnastics/kxWRuMBZjEVfUbdJjiVabM/story.html.

Radnofsky, Louise, and Cohen, Ben. "Rio 2016: How Simone Biles Crushed the Olympic Competition." *WSJ*, August 12, 2016. wsj.com/articles/rio-2016-simone-biles-takes-record-shattering-gold-in-womens-all-around-1470952167.

"Road to the Championships | NCAA.Com." NCAA.Com, October 22, 2018. ncaa.com/championships/gymnastics-women/nc/road-to-the-championship.

Ross, Ashley. "The Couple That Changed Gymnastics: 3 Decades of Karolyi Highlights." *Time,* August 8, 2016. time.com/4434463/history-bela-martha-karolyi/.

Sarkar, Pritha. "How an Unexpected Phone Call Put Biles on Path to Glory." Reuters, May 19, 2016. reuters.com/article/us-olympics-gymnastics-biles/how-an-unexpected-phone-call-put-biles-on-path-to-glory-idUSKCN0YA052.

"73 Questions with Simone Biles," September 15, 2016. youtube.com/watch?v-HHXRBItoqU.AtHome.

"Simone Biles—Academy of Achievement." Academy of Achievement, November 7, 2018. achievement.org/achiever/simone-biles/.

"Simone Biles Bio, Stats, and Results." Olympics at Sports-Reference.Com, n.d. sports-reference.com/olympics/athletes/bi/simone-biles-1.html.

"Simone Biles by the Numbers." SI.Com, September 15, 2016. si.com/olympics/2016/09/15/simone-biles-numbers-olympics-gymnastics-world-championships.

"Simone Biles USA." International Olympic Committee, December 18, 2018. olympic.org/simone-biles.

St. Clair, Stacy. "Aimee Boorman, Simone Biles' Chicago-Born Coach, Is Gymnastics' 'Ditka.'" Chicagotribune.com, August 14, 2016. chicagotribune.com/sports/international/ct-simone-biles-coach-aimee-boorman-olympics-spt-0815-20160814-story.html.

"Team USA Caps World Gymnastics Championships with Historic Medal Count." USA Gymnastics, October 2013. teamusa.org/News/2013/October/06/Team-USA-Caps-World-Gymnastics-Championships-With-Historic-Medal-Count.

"Simone Biles Crowned Gymnastics All-Around World Champion." Associated Press, October 4, 2013.

"20 Athletes with ADHD." Ranker, n.d. https://www.ranker.com/list/athletes-with-adhd/people-in-sports.

"20 Gymnastic Moves Explained in the Best Way Ever." SportsAspire, May 8, 2018. sportsaspire.com/gymnastic-moves.

"2017–2018 Women's Program Rules and Policies." USA Gymnastics, March 7, 2018. usagym.org/PDFs/Women/Rules/Rules%20and%20Policies/2017_2018_w_rulespolicies_0522.pdf.

"2018 U.S. Championships Results, Recaps, Photos, Videos." USA Gymnastics, n.d. usagym.org/pages/post.html?PostID=22434.

"USA Gymnastics | 2016 Olympic Games Results," USA Gymnastics, usagym.org/pages/events/2016/olympicsresults.html.

"USA Gymnastics | Junior Olympic Program Overview," USA Gymnastics, usagym.org/pages/women/pages/overview_jo.html.

"USA Gymnastics Names 2018—19 U.S. Women's National Team." USA Gymnastics, n.d. usagym.org/pages/post.html?PostID=22425&prog=h.

Van Deusen, Amy. "Gymnastics Vault: An Explosive and Exciting Apparatus." ThoughtCo, April 4, 2018. thoughtco.com/vault-1714816.

Van Deusen, Amy. "What Are the Basics of the Uneven Bars?" ThoughtCo, September 23, 2017. thoughtco.com/uneven-bars-1714815.

Van Deusen, Amy. "Who Are the Best Gymnastics Floor Workers in the World? Find Out Here." ThoughtCo, August 17, 2017. thoughtco.com/floor-exercise-1714813.

Wagoner, Mackenzie. "The Surprising Beauty Rules of USA Women's Gymnastics (or Why That Messy Ponytail Could Cost You a Penalty)." *Vogue*, May 26, 2017. vogue.com/article/2016-olympics-womens-gymnastics-rules-hair-jewelry-outfits-penalties.

Weiner, Zoë. "Simone Biles Just Made Her Debut as an NFL Cheerleader." *Teen Vogue*, December 11, 2017. teenvogue.com/story/simone-biles-honorary-texans-cheerleader.

"YouTube," May 12, 2016. youtube.com/watch?v=NCte7wP1R-8.

Wiedeman, Reeves. "Simone Biles Is the Best Gymnast in the World." The New Yorker, May 23, 2019. newyorker.com/magazine/2016/05/30/simone-biles-is-the-best-gymnast-in-the-world.

Zaccardi, Nick. "Simone Biles' Comeback Begins Where It All Started; How to Watch." OlympicTalk, July 25, 2018. olympics.nbcsports .com/2018/07/25/simone-biles-gymnastics-comeback-meet/.

Zaccardi, Nick. "World Gymnastics Championships Takeaways." OlympicTalk, October 10, 2017. olympics.nbcsports.com/2017/10/10/morgan-hurd-ragan-smith-gymnastics-world-championships/.

INDEX

IMAGE CREDITS

G.O.A.T.

STANDS FOR

GREATEST OF ALL TIME!

For athletes to be even considered the G.O.A.T. in their sport, it requires a lifelong dedication, nonstop hard work, and undeniable, unbelievable talent.

In this exciting new series— *G.O.A.T.: Making the Case for the Greatest of All Time*—we invite readers to analyze the facts, study the stats, and weigh in on the simple question ... Who is the true G.O.A.T.?

AVAILABLE NOW!

AVAILABLE SPRING 2020!

AVAILABLE FALL 2020!

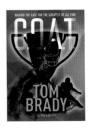

ISBN: 9781454932062

ISBN: 9781454930983

ISBN: 9781454932017

ISBN: 9781454930990